Feminism and its criticisms of traditional wives

Ingrid M. Taylor

Anuket Editorial

Contents:

Chapter 1
Historical Roots
of the Traditional Wife

What is a "traditional wife"?

The term "traditional wife" has gained relevance in recent years, especially in the realm of social media, generating debates and polarizing opinions. But what does it really mean to be a "traditional wife" in today's context?

A trip to the past:

To understand this concept, it is necessary to go back to historically established gender roles. In more traditional societies, women used to play a predominantly domestic role, taking care of household chores, raising children, and caring for their husbands. This model, although it has evolved, has left a deep mark on our culture and continues to be evoked by those who call themselves "traditional wives."

What does it mean to be a "traditional wife" today?

While there is no single, universal definition, "traditional wives" tend to share certain characteristics and values:

<u>Emphasis on the home</u>: Housework and caring for the family are considered fundamental priorities.

<u>Submission to the husband</u>: A hierarchy is accepted in the relationship, with the man making the important decisions.

<u>Conservative values:</u> They adhere to traditional values related to family, religion, and gender roles.

<u>Rejection of feminism:</u> Many "traditional wives" distance themselves from the feminist movement, arguing that its goals go against feminine nature.

An evolving concept:

It is important to note that the concept of "traditional wife" is not static, but rather adapts to social and cultural changes. What was understood as "traditional" a century ago is very different from what is considered today. In addition, the individual experiences of those who identify as "traditional wives" are diverse and cannot be generalized.

Criticisms and debates:

The concept of the "traditional wife" has been the subject of numerous criticisms. It is argued that:

<u>It reinforces gender stereotypes:</u> By perpetuating traditional gender roles, it limits women's opportunities and restricts them to the domestic sphere.

<u>It promotes unequal relationships:</u> Submission to the husband and lack of autonomy can generate

unbalanced relationships and harm women's well-being.

<u>It ignores the evolution of gender roles:</u> Denying the advances achieved by feminism and other social movements implies a regression in terms of equality.

Early Societies and the Rise of Patriarchy

In early human societies, gender-based divisions of labor arose from survival needs. Women, primarily responsible for childcare and food gathering, played a vital but subordinate role within the group. With sedentarization and the rise of agriculture, patriarchal structures were strengthened, where men controlled resources and political power.

Antiquity: Greece and Rome

In the civilizations of Greece and Rome, the figure of the wife was consolidated within a specific legal and social framework. In Athens, women were confined to the domestic sphere, under the guardianship of the men in their family. Marriage was seen as an institution for procreation and household management. In Rome, although women enjoyed more freedom than Greek women, their primary role was still to maintain the house and raise children.

The Middle Ages and Feudalism

During the Middle Ages, the feudal system reinforced traditional gender roles. Noble women had administrative responsibilities in their domains, but most women, especially peasant women, led a life centered on home and family. The Catholic Church also played a crucial role in consolidating the role of the wife as submissive and devoted to her husband, promoting the ideal of the virtuous and obedient woman.

Renaissance and Reformation: Changes and Continuities

The Renaissance brought cultural and social changes that affected expectations about women. Education for upper-class women began to be valued more, although it was still oriented toward preparation for marriage and household management. The Protestant Reformation also influenced the role of the wife, promoting marriage as an honorable state and the figure of the wife as the man's companion.

19th Century: The Victorian Wife

The 19th century, particularly the Victorian era, solidified the ideal of the wife as the angel of the home. Middle- and upper-class women were seen as guardians of morality and family stability, charged with creating a safe and virtuous haven for their husbands and children. This period also marked the beginning of feminist movements that began to question and challenge these traditional norms.

20th Century: Social Changes and the Challenge to the Traditional Role

The 20th century they have witnessed significant changes to the role of the traditional wife, driven by events such as the two World Wars and the Industrial Revolution. Women entered the workforce in droves, and the feminist movements of the 1960s and 1970s openly questioned traditional gender roles. Despite these changes, many women continued to choose traditional roles, and the debate over the role of the wife continued to evolve.

The figure of the traditional wife has changed significantly throughout history, reflecting movements in social, economic, and political structures. Understanding these historical roots is essential to contextualize modern critiques between feminists and traditional wives. This historical background provides a solid foundation for exploring the current dynamics between tradition and changing gender roles.

The debate on "traditional wives" invites us to reflect on the construction of gender roles, the evolution of the family, and the search for a balance between individual aspirations and collective responsibilities. It is essential to respect different ways of life, but also to question those practices that limit freedom and equal opportunities.

The role of the traditional wife has been a constant throughout human history, adapting to different cultural and social contexts. This chapter offers a tour of the evolution of this role, highlighting how it has been influenced by patriarchal structures and cultural norms of each era.

Chapter 2
The Tradwife Movement

The term "traditional wife" represents a subset of women who embrace traditional gender roles, focusing on full-time housework, child-rearing, and supporting their husbands, often at the expense of paid employment outside the home.

This lifestyle idealizes a nostalgic vision of 1950s America, characterized by nuclear families, well-defined gender roles, and a strong sense of community and tradition.

The traditional wife or "tradwife" movement has gained significant traction on social media platforms like TikTok, where influencers share content that romanticizes this lifestyle, serving as role models for younger generations despite prevailing progressive norms and the diverse gender roles of contemporary society.

However, the traditional wife movement is not without controversy. Critics argue that this lifestyle can be rigid and restrictive, potentially limiting personal growth and intimacy within relationships.

Furthermore, it is accused of aligning with far-right ideologies, subtly promoting conservative and white supremacist values under the guise of traditionalism.

While proponents claim that adopting this lifestyle is a personal and free choice, detractors worry about the broader implications and potential for propagating regressive social norms.

The tradwife movement is influenced by a complex interplay of personal, cultural, and religious factors. For some women, adopting this lifestyle provides an escape from the pressures of modern life, offering stability and simplicity.

Religious beliefs also play a role, with some tradwives seeing their lifestyle as a means of aligning themselves with biblical teachings and godly principles.

Social media has further popularized the movement, with influencers using platforms like TikTok, Instagram, and YouTube to share their daily lives, with influencers sharing content that idealizes this lifestyle. For example, in a TikTok video with over 1.6 million views, tradwife influencer Estee Williams explains that being a tradwife means embracing homemaking as their primary purpose and submitting to serving their husbands and families. Influencers use these platforms to share their daily lives, reinforcing traditional heteronormativity and gender roles in a visually appealing way.

These depictions serve as role models for younger generations, particularly Gen Z, who are being introduced to this lifestyle despite growing up in an era of greater progressivism and diverse gender roles. Reinforcing traditional gender roles in a visually appealing way inflames feminists who view such women as slaves to the patriarchy.

The movement has also received strong criticism for its stance against mainstream feminist ideologies. Traditional wives often take a stand against modern feminism, which they perceive as flawed and exclusionary.

Critics within the traditional wife community argue that feminism has strayed from its original goal of achieving equal rights and instead promotes ideologies that they see as oppressive and damaging to conventional femininity, womanhood, and motherhood.

This anti-feminist sentiment is a core element of the tradwife identity, reflecting broader societal debates about gender roles and nostalgia for a past that may never have really existed.

However, the traditional women's movement is not without controversy. Critics argue that the tradwife lifestyle can be rigid and restrictive, limiting personal growth and intimacy within relationships.

While proponents claim that adopting such a lifestyle is a free and personal choice, critics worry about the underlying implications and the potential for spreading regressive social norms.

Characteristics of Traditional Living

A modern traditional wife is defined by several key characteristics. First, there is a strong emphasis on traditional roles and duties, such as cooking, cleaning, and caring for the family. This is not seen as restrictive, but rather as a rewarding and valuable role.

A traditional wife places a high value on family values, often choosing to have more children and prioritizing their education over career ambitions.

Self-sufficiency is also important, with many traditional wives learning skills such as gardening, sewing, or food preservation.

Personality and personal preferences also play a role in the decision to adopt a traditional wife lifestyle. According to Power, Sensing, Judging, and Feeling, preferences may align with a traditional wife lifestyle due to its tendency toward practicality, structure, family, and tradition. Specific personality types such as ISFJ, ESFJ, ISTJ, and ESTJ are cited as logical alignments, though the reality is far more complex.

In traditional modern relationships, there is an emphasis on mutual respect and collaboration, recognizing that while roles may be traditional, both partners are equal. For those who practice this lifestyle, the division of roles does not make either partner subservient to the other.

This balance extends to various aspects of life, with traditional wives challenging the narrative that success can only be defined through professional achievements, proposing that personal fulfillment can also arise from family life and household chores.

Respect for marital vows is a crucial aspect, with a strong commitment to overcoming challenges rather than resorting to divorce.

On the other hand, social relationships outside the family unit can also be affected. Choosing to become a traditional wife can cause changes in friendships and could lead to judgments or misunderstandings from those who view the role from a different perspective.

The modern traditional wife often finds ways to integrate contemporary freedoms with classic values, amalgamating old-school beliefs with contemporary perspectives.

Influences and Inspirations

The traditional wife movement is influenced by a complex interplay of personal, cultural, and religious factors. For some women, adopting a traditional homemaker lifestyle serves as an escape from the pressures of modern life, offering a sense of stability and simplicity during turbulent times.

These motivations can vary widely, from a natural affinity for domestic roles to a desire for a more structured, faith-based life. A subset of traditional wives follow biblical teachings and view submission as a virtue and a way to align with divine principles.

Cultural norms and family background play a significant role in people's decision to adopt traditional gender roles. Licensed marriage and family therapist Rodman Walsh (Redondo Beach, CA) emphasizes that there is no "one size fits all" explanation for why people choose this lifestyle. Factors such as environment, community, and societal values significantly influence a person's belief system and perception of the world.

Some proponents of the traditional wives movement draw inspiration from historical and religious texts. The Bible, for example, is a cornerstone for many, offering verses that advocate traditional gender roles. Proverbs 31:26 is often cited for its emphasis on kindness and wisdom in the context of femininity.

Ellen White's book "The Adventist Home" further underscores the importance of mutual respect and cooperation between husband and wife, suggesting that traditional roles can foster harmony rather than subjugation.

Furthermore, the aesthetic and nostalgic appeal of the 1950s domestic ideal contributes to the movement's appeal. Influential traditional women often present an idyllic vision of domestic work, reminiscent of a time when women were primarily seen as homemakers. This nostalgic portrayal can be comforting to viewers, especially in today's fast-paced world.

However, critics argue that this romanticized view obscures the realities of women's submission and the potential for power imbalances in such relationships.

Faith-based motivations and a desire for stability are not the only drivers. Some women may turn to traditional roles as a means of dealing with personal or family trauma. For them, relinquishing control can feel empowering, as it offers a sense of security and order in an otherwise chaotic life. This phenomenon is particularly evident in times of social change, where the familiar and the firm become particularly attractive.

Chapter 3
Voices of Traditional Wives

The voices of traditional wives offer a unique and often underrepresented perspective in the debate on gender and feminism. This chapter explores the experiences, values, and motivations of women who choose to follow a traditional life path, in the context of a world that is rapidly changing towards gender equality and fluid roles.

Defining the Traditional Wife

Before diving into personal testimonies, we must remember the importance of understanding what a "traditional wife" encompasses. This term generally refers to women who take on conventional gender roles, centered on the home and family, and who often see caring for their husband and children as their primary responsibility.

Testimonies from Past Generations

Exploring the voices of traditional wives across different generations provides richer historical and cultural insight.

<u>Victorian Women</u>: Wives of this era often saw their role as angels of the home, dedicated to maintaining morale and family stability. This way of life is expressed in

letters and diaries of the time that reflected their thoughts and feelings.

20th Century Women: During the 1950s and 1960s, many women in Western countries embraced the ideal of the stay-at-home wife and mother. Through interviews and memoirs from that time, their experiences and how they perceived the social changes of the time are captured.

Contemporary Voices

They are mainly found on social media, where women transformed into influencers give current testimonies of those who choose to be traditional wives, despite the professional and educational opportunities available.

Personal Motivations: Many current women choose this role for religious, cultural, or personal reasons. Their testimonies are found not only in the mass media but also in daily relationships (shopping, school, entertainment), where they express their satisfaction and purpose in caring for their family and home.

The Influence of Faith: For some, religion plays a crucial role in their decision to follow a traditional path. Generally, in the practice of their religion, they express their vision of the assumed role as a spiritual vocation.

The Search for Balance: Some traditional wives today seek a balance between their family responsibilities and their personal or professional interests. They believe that they can have the best of both worlds, but their complaints of not being able to reach their full potential in either are also heard. Examples are women who run businesses from home or participate in community activities.

Values and Beliefs

Traditional wives often share certain values and beliefs that inform their life choices.

The Value of Family: Family is central in the lives of these women. Among themselves, they discuss their beliefs about the importance of a strong and stable family unit.

The Importance of Gender Roles: Many believe in the complementarity of traditional gender roles and see their role as essential to the harmonious functioning of the home.

Pride in Housework: Contrary to common perception, many traditional wives feel a deep pride and satisfaction in household chores and child-rearing.

Perceptions of Feminism

Traditional wives often have critical views on feminism, based on their own experiences and values.

Criticism of Devaluation of Domestic Role: Many feel that feminism often devalues domestic work and motherhood, promoting a limited view of female empowerment.

Impact on the Family: Some believe that feminism has contributed to the disintegration of the traditional family and has fostered a culture of individualism that runs counter to family values.

Perception of Freedom: While feminism strives for women's liberation, many traditional wives feel that their life choice is a legitimate form of freedom and autonomy.

Stories of Adaptation and Resistance

In the face of criticism, traditional wives have responded to social and cultural changes that promote gender equality.

Adaptation to New Realities: Some women find ways to adapt to modern expectations while maintaining their traditional values. For them, their stance is not rigid, as they are criticized for, but rather moldable to circumstances.

Resistance and Defense of Choice: This section of women fervently defend their life choices and fight against social pressure to conform to more progressive roles.

The voices of traditional wives offer a rich and nuanced perspective that is essential to understanding the debate on gender and feminism. Through their testimonies and experiences, the diversity of paths that women can choose and the importance of respecting and valuing all ways of life are highlighted. These stories also provide vital context for the critiques of feminism that will be explored in the following chapters.

Notable Figures

Estee Williams

Estee Williams is one of the most prominent figures in the traditional wives movement, which has gained significant attention on platforms such as TikTok. Known for her 1950s-inspired housewife lifestyle, she regularly shares clips of herself getting ready for her husband's return from work by doing things like styling her hair, applying red lipstick, and changing into floral dresses, all set to nostalgic music.

Her TikTok videos, which capture a day in her life as a traditional wife, garner hundreds of thousands of views and tens of thousands of likes.

Estee's depiction of the traditional wife lifestyle embodies the movement's emphasis on traditional gender roles and domestic duties.

Hannah Neeleman

Another major influencer within the traditional wife community is Hannah Neeleman, who operates under the username @ballerinafarm on Instagram. With over

9 million followers, she showcases her life as a mother of eight on a farm in Utah. Despite her association with the traditional wife movement by the public, Neeleman does not identify with the term.

She has been featured in the UK's The Sunday Times, offering a detailed look at her daily life, which includes elaborate home-cooked meals and a 1950s-inspired wardrobe.

Her dynamic with her husband, Daniel, adheres to traditional roles, which she describes as "a man and a woman" working together.

However, critics point out that her description of the lifestyle omits her husband's significant inherited wealth, painting a somewhat skewed picture of the existence of traditional wives.

Alena Kate Pettitt
Alena Kate Pettitt is another influential figure in the traditional wives movement, advocating for traditional family values through her writing and online presence. Pettitt is the author of "The Darling Academy" etiquette books and articles, where she criticizes modern media for destroying traditional family values and promoting the traditional wives' lifestyle.

She highlights the importance of traditional gender roles and often provides advice on how women can embrace these roles in their marriages.

Laura

A self-proclaimed traditional wife, Laura has taken part in several interviews to defend her lifestyle choice. In an interview with ABC News Australia, she shared her reasons for adopting the traditional wife lifestyle, highlighting her desire to stay home with her children rather than leave them in the care of someone else.

Laura's story is emblematic of many women in the traditional wives movement who feel a deep connection to the role of full-time homemaker and mother.

RoRo Bueno

Spanish influencer with more than 3 million followers on TikTok. From uploading videos of her daily life and gym tips, she became world famous when, with her high-pitched voice, she commented that for that day she was preparing a special meal for her boyfriend Pablo, which he had asked her for. Faced with the fury unleashed by feminists, who accused her of subordinating herself to her partner's requests, RoRo's videos began to go viral. The influencer already has more than a million followers on Instagram and around 50 million views on some of her most popular videos. However, in recent times she began to receive a series of criticisms due to the lifestyle she advocates.

She is a promoter of the "tradwife" movement promoting traditional gender roles. The 22-year-old shows her day-to-day life in which she dedicates herself to making elaborate preparations in her charming and tidy kitchen.

Chapter 4
Criticism of the Tradwife Movement

Public perception and controversy

The tradwife movement has garnered a mix of support and criticism, with perceptions often divided along ideological lines. Advocates argue that the movement is a reaction to the social displacement felt by young people today as they struggle to find their place and value in a rapidly changing world.

Its members vehemently deny any association with far-right ideologies and claim not to support anything resembling white supremacy.

However, critics argue that the movement often glorifies a mythical postwar 1950s American culture, characterized by predominantly white nuclear families, which serves as a coded language for demographic panic and a call to restore a conservative, homogenous American identity.

This representation has led some to compare Tradwives to supporters of laws like Florida's "Don't Say Gay" bill, which seeks to return society to what some perceive as a simpler time with fewer individual freedoms.

The "Don't Say Gay" Act is a collection of more than 150 anti-LGBT bills introduced at the state level, ranging from restricting access to gender-affirming health care for minors to excluding transgender children from athletics. Other bills up for passage include a Georgia bill similar to the Florida bill that restricts discussion of LGBT issues, and another Idaho bill that could punish medical personnel who provide gender-affirming health care, and parents who agree to their children receiving such care, with up to life in prison.

Psychology professor Noam Shpancer of the Center for Cognitive and Behavioral Therapy in Columbus, Ohio, suggests that this traditional trend could be a reaction to the general liberalization of American belief systems, as each new generation becomes more open about race, sexuality, and gender.

There is concern, however, about the movement's simplistic and often stereotypical portrayal of traditional culture, which some believe is more influenced by media depictions than historical reality.

Critics, such as Stanford University trauma specialist Dr. Paul Conti, warn that such curated messages around dependency and feminine roles are not rooted in reality and could undermine individual agency and resilience.

In addition, the tradwife movement has faced backlash for its potential alignment with extremist ideologies. Far-right men from Generation Z in particular have embraced the concept of aggressive heterosexuality and machismo, using the attack on women as a way to assert their dominance. This has created an exclusionary environment in far-right youth groups, further complicating the public perception of the traditional wives' movement

Ultimately, the traditional wives phenomenon underscores a broader societal debate about gender roles, identity, and nostalgia for an idealized past. While social media continues to amplify extreme examples, the challenge remains to promote more egalitarian models of marriage and family life that resonate with the complexities of modern society.

Chapter 5
Understanding Patriarchy

The history of patriarchy traces the development of a social system in which men predominantly hold power and women are largely excluded from it, from ancient times to the present day.

Originating in early human societies, patriarchy was accentuated by the advent of agriculture, property ownership, and urbanization. This shift entrenched male dominance, as codified in early legal codes and religious texts, creating enduring social structures that have influenced several civilizations and historical periods.

In ancient civilizations, such as those of the Near East, the Indus Valley, China, and Mesoamerica, patriarchal norms were consolidated through social and technological advances. Anthropological evidence suggests that earlier egalitarian structures gave way to patriarchal systems as societies became more complex. Classical antiquity, particularly in Greece and Rome, saw the entrenchment of patriarchal ideologies, which were further reinforced by philosophers such as Aristotle and legal systems that codified gender roles.

During the medieval and early modern periods, patriarchy became intertwined with economic, political, cultural, and religious structures. Women's roles were largely confined to the domestic sphere, with limited economic and social autonomy. Despite these restrictions, instances where women wielded significant power within their households and communities reveal the complexity of patriarchal systems.

The rise of capitalism and urbanization in this era further reinforced patriarchal norms, although some women found new opportunities for independence through wage labor.

The 19th and 20th centuries marked significant challenges to patriarchal structures, driven by industrialization and feminist movements. Women increasingly entered the workforce, fought for legal rights, and challenged traditional gender norms. The women's suffrage movement, which culminated in the early twentieth century, and the second wave of feminism in the 1960s and 1970s, sought broader gender equality and legislative reforms. Despite progress, ongoing criticism highlights the persistent gender pay gap, underrepresentation in leadership roles, and the double burden of professional and domestic responsibilities, underscoring the need for continued efforts to achieve gender equity.

Origins of Patriarchy

Patriarchy refers to a social system in which men predominantly hold power, and has been a crucial category for social analysis in feminist theory and theology. The term "patriarchy" itself means the rule of the father as the fundamental principle of social organization within the family and society at large.

Patriarchal systems appear to have first emerged among nomadic pastoralist groups between the tenth and fifth millennium BCE. C. in several regions, including the ancient Near East, the Indus Valley, China, and Mesoamerican cultures.

As these societies moved from nomadic lifestyles to sedentary agricultural communities, patriarchal structures became more pronounced. This shift was marked by the move to larger-scale agriculture, land ownership, and urbanization. By the third millennium BCE, written legal codes had emerged that further cemented patriarchal norms.

The commodification of women's sexual and reproductive capacities, which coincided with the development of private property, played a major role in establishing patriarchal social structures. This historical development set the stage for male dominance and control over women.

The Bible, particularly in stories such as that of Adam and Eve, is often cited as an early example of patriarchal ideology, where the creation of Adam before Eve positions him as the dominant figure.

Evidence from Ancient Civilizations

Anthropological, archaeological, and evolutionary psychological evidence suggests that most prehistoric societies were relatively egalitarian. Patriarchal social structures did not develop until after the end of the

Pleistocene, following social and technological advances such as agriculture and domestication.

For example, administrative tablets from the Sumerian city of Uruk in ancient Mesopotamia, dating back about 5,000 years, provide the first clear signs that women were treated categorically differently than men.

These tablets indicate a deliberate effort to enumerate populations and resources, reflecting the beginning of institutionalized gender roles. In Ming Dynasty China, patriarchal norms were deeply rooted in Confucian ideals, according to which widowed women were expected to remain single and chaste for life. Women who adhered to these ideals were celebrated and sometimes had structures erected in their honor.

In contrast, in ancient Egypt, middle-class women enjoyed a greater degree of autonomy, as they participated in trade, real estate transactions, and even legal processes. The contrast between the roles of Egyptian and Athenian women highlights the variability of patriarchal systems across cultures.

The shift from matriarchy to patriarchy

The idea that matriarchy preceded patriarchy in human societies was posited by 19th-century social evolutionists such as Friedrich Engels and J. J. Bachofen. This idea was later taken up by feminist scholars in the 1970s. For example, archaeologist Marija Gimbutas suggested that the peaceful, egalitarian, gynocentric Neolithic societies of Europe were overthrown by patriarchal invaders during the Bronze Age.

This theory, though contested, highlights the complex and varied history of social organization and gender roles in early human societies. At the archaeological site of Çatalhöyük, dating back some 9,000 years in present-day Turkey, evidence points to a relatively egalitarian society in which gender had little importance in everyday life.

Patriarchy in Classical Antiquity

Patriarchy as a social system is found in classical societies around the world. Some anthropologists, such as Elman Service, believe that the patriarchal family was the aboriginal order of human society and is therefore "natural" and inevitable. However, feminist anthropologists have challenged this assumption, arguing that patriarchal systems emerged at a particular time in human history with the transition from food gathering and horticulture to plow farming, private land ownership, urbanization, and class stratification.

In the ancient Near East, this shift occurred sometime between the seventh and fourth millennium BCE and shaped the patriarchal ideological and social patterns of classical societies and the religious cultures of the Hebrews, Greeks, and Romans.

In ancient Greece, patriarchal norms were evident in social structures and cultural practices. Although many 16th- and 17th-century theorists concurred with

Aristotle's views on women's place in society, patriarchal political theory did not take hold until after the publication of Sir Robert Filmer's Patriarcha sometime before 1653, which argued for the divine right of kings based on male lineage from Adam.

Greek influence spread with the conquests of Alexander the Great, further consolidating these patriarchal norms.

The Greek philosopher Plato, in his work The Republic, offered a counterpoint by imagining a society in which women would have complete educational and political equality and serve in the military. However, this vision was not widely adopted in practice.

In contrast, Plato's disciple Aristotle held more traditional views on gender roles, which contributed to the patriarchal sentiment prevalent in classical Greece. This was exemplified by the Athenian family model, which became widely accepted throughout Greek societies. Despite social restrictions, Greek women found ways to work around these limitations, but the social structure remained predominantly patriarchal.

The influence of patriarchy extended to Roman society as well. Roman law codified patriarchal structures, which were reflected in family and legal practices. Women's roles were confined to the domestic sphere, although they could own property and engage in business transactions under certain conditions.

References to matrilineal societies in pre-classical Europe, such as those found in ruins dating to 7000

BC on the Aegean and Adriatic coasts, suggest that earlier social structures may have been less patriarchal. These societies, characterized by peaceful, stable villages with significant female iconography, contrast sharply with later patriarchal systems that emerged with greater social stratification and institutionalized violence.

Medieval Period

During the medieval period, the structure of patriarchy in European society continued to evolve, becoming intertwined with economic, political, cultural, and religious issues. The economic institutions that emerged in the Middle Ages, such as craft guilds, were notably patriarchal. Women were generally excluded from formal apprenticeship programs leading to independent mastery within a guild. However, women could sometimes work in a shop if they were the wife or daughter of a master, and could even run a shop as a master's widow. This arrangement meant that a woman's ability to work depended on her relationship to a man, rather than her skills and training. Even within guilds, a patriarchal hierarchy existed in which masters had authority over their apprentices and journeymen, who were often adult men.

Patriarchy in the medieval period extended beyond economic institutions into diverse social relationships. Government relations from the 15th to the 18th century were distinctly patriarchal, encompassing husbands and wives, parents and children, masters and servants, pastors and parishioners, rulers and subjects, and sometimes employers and workers. The multifaceted nature of early modern patriarchy made it appear as an inevitable and natural part of life, perceived as God-given and natural. Consequently, those perceived as opposed to or subverted by patriarchy were often depicted and sometimes treated very harshly.

In the religious context, Church Fathers such as St. Augustine promoted the concept of male headship, leading to the belief that women lacked the image of God in themselves and could only be included in the image of God under their husbands as their "head." Women were seen as naturally subjugated and inferior, more prone to sin, lacking reason and self-control, and defined by their bodies and sexuality. As such, women were seen as incapable of representing Christ in ordained ministry. These views stemmed from the patriarchal patterns built into Christian theology and church polity.

Despite these prevailing patriarchal norms, there were instances where women held considerable power within the home, even in traditions officially structured to promote male authority. For example, in 19th-century Italian-American Catholicism, there was a public patriarchy but a private matriarchy. Similarly, conservative Protestants officially promoted male authority, but women founded and led popular movements, particularly in early Pentecostalism and healing ministries. This distinction between public (official) and private (domestic) roles demonstrates the complexity of patriarchal structures within religious contexts.

Early Modern Period

During the Early Modern Period, from the 15th to the 18th century, patriarchy was explicitly institutionalized in Western Europe. This era witnessed the establishment of a father-centered social structure, where relationships such as husbands and wives, parents and children, masters and servants, rulers and subjects were distinctly patriarchal.

The multifaceted nature of early modern patriarchy made it appear as an inevitable part of life, often regarded as God-given and natural. Consequently, those who were perceived as opposed to or subverted by this structure were treated harshly.

The cultural and religious norms of the time significantly accentuated gender distinctions. As farming communities evolved and developed irrigation systems and buildings, they began to see themselves as separate from and superior to the natural world, thus fostering a nature-culture dichotomy. Women, who were primarily the bearers of children and did not own irrigated fields, were increasingly considered closer to nature and therefore inferior. As their work became more confined to the domestic sphere, men, whose work was done outside the home and in cooperation with other men, were associated with the public sphere, which grew in complexity and importance as communities and states expanded.

The interrelationship of capitalism and patriarchy did not affect all of Europe uniformly, nor did it affect all social groups in the same way. The expansion of wage labor, despite its low pay and status, actually benefited some women by allowing them to leave their parental homes and potentially support themselves without marrying. However, political authorities found this possibility of greater independence unacceptable and began passing laws that forced women to work in male-headed households. For example, in southern Germany, unmarried women were prohibited from moving to cities unless they engaged in domestic service in a household headed by a man. A pejorative term, Eigenbrötlerinnen (women who earn their bread), was used for women who lived independently.

The economic and political changes of this period were reinforced by cultural and religious concepts that emphasized gender distinctions. These developments contributed to the establishment and maintenance of a patriarchal society in which women's roles were predominantly domestic, while men dominated the public sphere. This dichotomy continued to shape social norms and expectations well into the following centuries.

Events of the 19th Century

The 19th century marked significant transformations in social structures and gender roles, particularly with the onset of industrialization and the rise of feminist movements. During this period, industrialization redefined women's roles both in the home and in the workplace. Before industrialization, the home was the center of production in preindustrial America, where men and women contributed equally to family survival through agricultural labor and household production.

However, industrialization opened up new opportunities for women as wage earners in factories and industries, particularly in textile and garment factories, leading to greater economic independence.

Around the same time, the feminist movement began to take shape, advocating for gender equality and women's rights. Feminist activists demanded legal reforms to guarantee women's property rights, divorce rights, and employment opportunities. A notable milestone was the Seneca Falls Convention in 1848, where the Declaration of Sentiments was adopted, demanding equal rights for women in various aspects of life.

Despite these efforts, progress was slow and women continued to face significant barriers and prejudices throughout the century.

The 19th century also saw the rise of the women's suffrage movement, spearheaded by activists such as Susan B. Anthony and Elizabeth Cady Stanton. They fought for women's right to vote and for greater political equality, ultimately culminating in the passage of the Nineteenth Amendment to the U.S. Constitution in 1920, which granted women the right to vote.

Literature and writing served as powerful tools of resistance against patriarchy, and authors such as Jane Austen, Charlotte Brontë, and Mary Wollstonecraft used their works to challenge societal norms and advocate for women's rights and independence.

Throughout the century, feminist thought evolved, challenging traditional gender norms and promoting the idea that gender roles were social constructs and therefore mutable. Feminists such as Kate Millett argued that gender roles reinforced women's subordination and needed to be dismantled through social and political reforms aimed at creating more equal societies.

This perspective laid the groundwork for future feminist movements that sought to unlearn these socially constructed roles and diminish the influence of gender-based socialization.

20th Century

The 20th century marked significant changes and challenges to traditional patriarchal structures. The women's suffrage movement gained momentum and culminated in the granting of voting rights to women in many countries. This was a fundamental step in redefining gender roles and improving women's participation in public life. However, the road to gender equality was far from over.

Women's Participation in the Workforce

During the first decades of the 20th century, women's roles continued to be largely defined by domestic responsibilities. However, the Industrial Revolution had already laid the groundwork for women to participate more actively in the workforce. By the beginning of the 20th century, a significant number of women were working in various sectors, although they were often relegated to lower-paid and less prestigious jobs. The onset of the world wars saw women enter the workforce in unprecedented numbers, taking on roles that had traditionally been filled by men due to labor shortages caused by the wars.

These changes began to alter societal perceptions of women's abilities and roles.

The post-war period and second-wave feminism

After the Second World War, many women were expected to return to domestic roles. However, the seeds of change had already been sown. In the 1960s and 1970s, the second wave of feminism emerged, focusing on a broader range of issues beyond suffrage, such as equality in the workplace, reproductive rights, and the dismantling of traditional gender roles.

Feminists argued that gender roles were a social construct and could be changed to create a more equitable society. This era saw significant legislative changes, such as the introduction of equal pay and anti-discrimination laws in several countries.

Changing gender norms

The second half of the 20th century saw further changes in gender norms. Educational opportunities for women expanded, and more women opted to pursue higher education and professional careers.

Despite these advances, women continued to face significant challenges, such as the gender pay gap and underrepresentation in leadership positions. The feminist movement of this period also drew attention to issues such as sexual harassment and violence against women, further challenging patriarchal structures.

Continuing criticism and challenges

Despite the progress made, criticism of patriarchal structures persists. Feminists highlight the double burden faced by many women, who are expected to excel in their professional lives while also taking care of domestic responsibilities.

This "double burden" underscores the need for a more equitable distribution of domestic work and the importance of supportive policies such as parental leave and affordable childcare.

Chapter 6
Feminism and its Waves

Feminism, as a social and political movement, has gone through several stages known as "waves." Each of these waves has addressed different issues related to gender equality, adapting to the historical and cultural contexts of its time. This chapter traces the evolution of feminism, highlighting its main achievements and key figures, to provide a frame of reference for the critiques addressed in the book.

The First Wave: 19th and Early 20th Centuries

The first wave of feminism focused primarily on women's legal and political rights, with a strong emphasis on women's suffrage.

Historical Context: It emerged in the 19th century, in a period of significant social and political change, including the Industrial Revolution and civil rights movements.

Main Demands: The right to vote, women's education, and equality before the law.

Key Figures: Mary Wollstonecraft, Sojourner Truth, Susan B. Anthony, Elizabeth Cady Stanton.

Significant Achievements: Passage of the 19th Amendment in the United States (1920), which granted women the right to vote, and similar advances in other Western countries.

The Second Wave: 1960s and 1970s

Second-wave feminism broadened its focus to include a wide range of social, cultural, and economic issues.

Historical Context: Born in the context of the civil rights movements, the 1960s counterculture, and the peace movement.

Key Demands: Equal pay and employment, reproductive rights, and the elimination of gender discrimination in all spheres of life.

Key Figures: Betty Friedan, Gloria Steinem, Simone de Beauvoir.

Significant Achievements: The Equal Pay Act (1963), the creation of the Women's Civil Rights Commission, the legalization of abortion in several countries, and the implementation of affirmative action policies.

The Third Wave: 1990s and 2000s

The third wave of feminism was characterized by its diversity and its focus on intersectionality.

Historical Context: It emerged in a globalized world with a growing awareness of differences in race, class, sexuality, and other identities.

<u>Key Demands</u>: Greater inclusion and representation of women from different backgrounds, broader approaches to sexuality, and the fight against gender violence.

<u>Key Figures:</u> Rebecca Walker, Kimberlé Crenshaw, bell hooks.

<u>Significant Achievements:</u> Development of theories of intersectionality, increased representation of women in media and politics, and greater legal protections against domestic violence and sexual harassment.

The Fourth Wave: 2010 onwards

The fourth wave of feminism has been characterized by the use of digital technologies and a renewed focus on social justice and human rights.

It is developing in the context of the digital age, with the extensive use of social media and a growing global awareness of persistent inequalities.

Its demands include ending sexual harassment and gender violence, equality in the workplace, and the recognition of rights for all gender identities.

Its key figures include Malala Yousafzai, Tarana Burke (founder of the #MeToo movement), and Emma Watson.

Its most significant achievements include the birth of global movements such as #MeToo and Time's Up, progressive legislation on gender equality, and greater recognition and support for LGBTQ+ people.

This fourth wave of feminism has burst onto the global social and political landscape, redefining the parameters of the debate on gender equality. This movement, characterized by its diversity and intersectional approach, seeks to address structural inequalities that persist, not only in terms of gender but also race, class, sexual orientation, and gender identity.

The relationship between fourth-wave feminism and the woke movement is complex and often debated. Both movements share several common goals, such as fighting discrimination, promoting social justice, and deconstructing systems of oppression. However, there are also significant differences in their approaches and priorities.

Similarities between both movements

Intersectionality: Both fourth-wave feminism and the woke movement recognize the importance of addressing the multiple forms of oppression that people experience. This involves understanding how gender intersects with other social identities, such as race, class, and sexual orientation, to create unique experiences of oppression.

Deconstruction of power systems: Both movements seek to question and dismantle the patriarchal, racist, and capitalist systems of power that perpetuate inequality.

<u>Use of social media:</u> Social media has been central to both movements, allowing for the organization, mobilization, and dissemination of ideas on a global level.

Differences between the two movements

<u>Emphasis:</u> While fourth-wave feminism focuses on the experiences of women and girls, the woke movement has a broader focus that includes a variety of marginalized identities and experiences.

<u>Language and terminology:</u> The woke movement has introduced new terms and concepts into public debate, such as "microaggressions," "privilege," and "cancellation." These terms are not always used in the same way within fourth-wave feminism.

<u>Strategies:</u> The two movements employ different strategies to achieve their goals. Fourth-wave feminism has used both traditional tactics, such as organizing marches and protests, and more novel strategies, such as creating safe spaces online. The woke movement, on the other hand, has placed a greater emphasis on education and awareness-raising.

Challenges and Criticisms

Both fourth-wave feminism and the woke movement face several challenges and criticisms. Some of the main challenges include:

<u>Internal Division:</u> Both movements are internally diverse and debates often arise over issues of strategy, identity, and language.

<u>Accusations of Essentialism:</u> Critics argue that both movements sometimes fall into essentialism, reducing people's experiences to a set of fixed characteristics.

<u>Cancel Cultures:</u> The woke movement has been accused of fostering a cancel culture, where people are quickly judged and condemned online for words or actions perceived as offensive.

<u>Criticisms of Intersectionality:</u> The lack of representation and consideration of women of different races, classes, and sexual orientations in the early waves.

<u>Debates on Sexuality:</u> Differences in perspectives on sexuality and sex work.

<u>Generational Conflicts:</u> Differences between feminists of different generations over priorities and methods of struggle.

Fourth-wave feminism and the woke movement can be seen as two powerful forces that are transforming the social and political landscape. While they share many common goals, there are also significant differences in their approaches and priorities. It is important to recognize both the similarities and differences between these movements to better understand the complexities of social activism today.

Chapter 7
Major Criticisms of Feminism

Feminism has been a powerful force for social change, fighting for gender equality and women's rights. However, not all women view feminism positively. This chapter explores the main criticisms of feminism from the perspective of traditional wives, analyzing their arguments and the reasons behind their views.

The Devaluation of the Domestic Role

A common criticism is that feminism has devalued domestic work and the role of wife and mother.

Since second-wave feminism, the idea has been promoted that true women's empowerment lies in participation in the workforce and in gaining economic independence.

Traditional wives argue that this view has led to a decrease in respect for domestic work and child-rearing, roles they consider essential to family and social stability.

The Importance of Motherhood

Feminism has promoted choice and autonomy in all aspects of women's lives, including motherhood.

Many traditional wives believe that feminism has downplayed the importance of motherhood, often presenting it as a less valuable option or as an obstacle to personal fulfillment.

For these women, motherhood is a central part of their identity and personal fulfillment. They view raising children as a noble and crucial task that should be respected and supported.

There is also criticism of Feminist Policies; most notably how some feminist policies, although well-intentioned, can be perceived as discouraging motherhood, such as promoting abortion and birth control without sufficient emphasis on supporting mothers.

The Gender Divide

Some traditional wives argue that feminism has fostered gender division and conflict.

They note how certain strands of radical feminism can be seen as antagonistic towards men, promoting a narrative of conflict rather than collaboration. Traditional wives often value the idea of complementary gender roles, where men and women have different, but equally important responsibilities.

Lack of Representation and Diversity

Another criticism is that feminism sometimes fails to adequately represent all women, especially those who choose traditional roles.

Although third-wave feminism has attempted to address intersectionality, some traditional wives feel that their experiences and choices are not sufficiently represented or respected within the movement.

It is argued that feminism should be more inclusive and recognize that the fight for equality must also include respect for traditional life choices.

The Impact on Family Structure

Traditional wives often believe that feminism has hurt family structure.

When looking at the correlation between the rise of feminism and divorce rates, it is argued that the emphasis on individual independence can undermine marital commitment.

Traditional women note how family dynamics have changed with feminism, including the rise of single-parent families and the negative impact on children.

Responses to Criticisms

For their part, feminists have responded to criticisms against them, including the need for a more inclusive understanding of feminism.

Contemporary feminism responds to these criticisms by promoting the idea that women should be free to choose their path, whether in the home or their professional careers.

They propose how feminism can work to support both women who choose professional careers and those who opt for traditional roles.

The Tradwives movement, characterized by a return to traditional gender roles and domesticity, is often positioned in opposition to dominant feminist ideologies. A primary criticism voiced by Tradwives is directed at modern feminism, which they perceive as flawed and toxic. Some argue that the core tenets of feminism are tainted and historically exclusionary, citing figures such as Elizabeth Cady Stanton, who promoted the rights of white women but excluded women of color.

Anti-feminist sentiments within the Tradwife community are also rooted in the belief that feminism has strayed from its original goal of achieving equal rights. True feminism should advocate for equal rights and responsibilities for both men and women without seeking special privileges for women.

Furthermore, Tradwives often criticize the various waves of feminism for promoting ideologies they view as oppressive. They reject first--, second-, and third-wave feminism, seeing them as attacks on traditional femininity, womanhood, and motherhood. Fourth-wave feminism, which emphasizes empowerment, online advocacy, and movements like #MeToo, is perceived by many right-leaning Tradwives as a man-hating ideology.

Some scholars on the topic suggest that Tradwives' anti-feminist stance is a reaction to what they see as the failings of liberal feminism. While liberal feminism encouraged middle-class women to join the workforce as a means of emancipation, the toxic nature of many workplaces has made this promise seem unfulfilled for some women. Consequently, Tradwifes often blame feminism for structural problems like crises in childcare and overwork rather than recognizing them as broader societal issues.

Furthermore, the Tradwife movement's critique of feminism extends to the notion of "choice feminism," which is criticized for justifying individual life choices without addressing broader social structures. These critics highlight that, despite the progress made, women still face disproportionate rates of sexual violence, earn less than men, and often take on more domestic work even when they earn more than their husbands. This critique underscores a perceived disconnect between feminist rhetoric and the lived realities of many women

Related Movements and Concepts

The anger and helplessness young people feel in the face of societal breakdown are justified by current trends, but these emotions also make them vulnerable to dangerous movements that offer simplified explanations for an increasingly complex world. As Dr. Eviane Leidig from Tilburg University in the Netherlands, a researcher on far-right, gender, and online radicalization, explains in a 2020 Impakter article, "From Incels to Tradwives," young men and women are drawn to far-right ideologies because these movements simplify a convoluted reality, taking refuge in chat rooms and algorithmic recommendations.

This nostalgia for a mythical past, where gender norms and social status were clearly defined, displaces the anxiety young people feel about societal collapse onto concerns about relationships and gender.

This shifting view of masculinity has sparked an intense backlash among far-right Gen Z men. Young white male nationalists invest heavily in male chauvinism and aggressive heterosexuality to distance themselves from what they perceive as their generation's moral decay. Attacks on women and slut-shaming to assert dominance are prevalent in paleoconservative Christian Zoom and white nationalist circles, where women are often excluded, as evidenced by America First leader Nick Fuentes' unofficial mantra: "No e-girls, ever!"

As we see, critiques of feminism from the perspective of traditional wives are varied and complex, reflecting a rich diversity of experiences and values. It is noted that between the two positions, there are voices that often feel marginalized in the discourse on gender equality. By recognizing and respecting these voices, we can work towards a more inclusive and understanding movement that embraces all forms of female life and choice.

Chapter 8
The Debate on Choice and Autonomy

The concept of autonomy and choice has been central to both feminism and traditional wives. However, how this autonomy is understood and valued can vary significantly between the two groups. This chapter examines these differences, offering a historical overview of the debate on choice and autonomy in the context of gender roles.

Origins of the Debate

The debate on choice and autonomy has deep roots in the history of the feminist movement and the defense of traditional gender roles.

First Wave Feminism

During the first wave, feminists fought for the right to vote, education, and participation in public life. Autonomy was primarily understood as access to the same rights and opportunities as men.

Traditional Counterpart: At the same time, many women continued to see their role in the home as a valid and valuable choice, a form of autonomy in their sphere of influence.

Second Wave and Individual Autonomy

Second-wave feminism brought a more intense focus on individual autonomy and women's liberation from traditional gender roles.

Criticism of the Domestic Role: Second-wave feminists argued that the domestic role and compulsory motherhood were forms of oppression. The idea that true freedom lay in participation in the workforce and economic independence was promoted.

Traditional Responses: Many traditional wives responded by defending their choice to focus on home and family. They argued that this choice was a form of autonomy that should be respected and valued.

Third Wave and Diversity of Choices

Third-wave feminism introduced a greater awareness of the diversity of life experiences and choices.

Intersectionality and Choice: Third-wave feminists began to recognize that women have different backgrounds and priorities. Choosing to be a homemaker could be a valid form of empowerment for some.

Traditional Voices: During this period, more traditional women's voices began to be heard, highlighting the importance of recognizing and respecting all forms of female autonomy.

The Fourth Wave and the Digital Age

The fourth wave of feminism has used social media and digital platforms to broaden the debate about autonomy and choice.

Online Movements: Movements such as #MeToo have placed a strong emphasis on bodily autonomy and women's freedom to make decisions about their own lives and bodies.

Social Media Debate: Traditional wives have also used these platforms to share their stories and defend their choice of traditional roles. Social media has provided a space for the exchange of ideas and mutual respect.

Criticisms and Challenges

The debate about choice and autonomy has generated criticism and challenges on both sides.

Criticisms of Feminism: Traditional wives criticize feminism for not adequately valuing traditional life choices. They argue that feminism sometimes imposes a single vision of empowerment that does not include the value of domestic work and motherhood.

Criticisms of Traditional Roles: On the other hand, feminists argue that traditional roles can limit women's autonomy, perpetuating inequalities and economic dependencies.

<u>We must consider the following:</u> feminism is a movement as diverse as society itself and is in a constant process of evolution and debate. One of the hottest topics today is that of women's "choice and autonomy," a debate that has generated tensions between the most radical and the most traditional currents.

On the one hand, radical feminists defend the absolute freedom of women to make decisions about their bodies and their lives, without external interference. They advocate the right to abortion, sexual freedom, and reproductive autonomy as fundamental pillars of gender equality. For them, any restriction on these freedoms is a form of patriarchal oppression.

On the other hand, more traditional women, although also defenders of women's rights, have certain reservations regarding some of the postulates of radical feminists. Although they recognize the importance of female autonomy, they consider that there are limits that must be respected, such as the protection of life from conception or the importance of the family as an institution.

Where are the points of friction between these two positions?

<u>Abortion:</u> The issue of abortion is undoubtedly the most controversial. While radical feminists consider it a fundamental right, more traditional women often see it as a practice that should be regulated or even prohibited.

<u>Sexuality:</u> Sexual freedom is another issue that generates debate. Radical feminists advocate the decriminalization of all consensual sexual practices between adults, while more traditional women may show some reluctance towards some practices considered "deviant" or "immoral".

<u>Motherhood:</u> Motherhood is a central aspect of many women's lives. While radical feminists defend the right of women to choose whether or not to be mothers, more traditional women often see motherhood as a natural vocation and an essential element of personal fulfillment.

Is it possible to find common ground?

Despite the differences, it is important to highlight that both radical feminists and more traditional women share a common goal: equal opportunities for women. The key to finding common ground lies in dialogue and mutual respect.

It is necessary to recognize that each woman's experience is unique and that there is no single answer that is valid for all questions. Feminism must be an inclusive movement, capable of welcoming women with different beliefs and values.

In this sense, it is essential to promote an open and respectful debate, in which all voices are heard and consensual solutions are sought. Only through dialogue can we build a stronger and more representative feminism.

In conclusion, the debate on "choice and autonomy" is a reflection of the complexity of feminism as a movement. While there are tensions between the different currents, it is essential to remember that they all share the same goal: the liberation of women. Through dialogue and mutual respect, we can find a path towards a more equal future for all.

The debate over choice and autonomy is complex and multifaceted, reflecting a rich diversity of experiences and values. Both feminist and traditional wives seek autonomy for women, although they understand and value this autonomy in different ways. By exploring these perspectives, this chapter offers a more complete view of the debate, promoting mutual respect and understanding.

Chapter 9
Emerging movements
and changes in social paradigms

In recent decades, feminism has played a central role in the transformation of relations between men and women. Since its emergence, feminism has evolved in different waves and currents, each with a particular focus, but with the common goal of promoting gender equality and challenging patriarchal structures. At the same time, movements have emerged that react to these positions, generating a substantial change in the way men and women relate today.

Changes driven by feminist positions

<u>Demanding rights and autonomy:</u> Feminist movements have been crucial in expanding rights for women, such as the right to vote, access to education and employment opportunities, as well as the right to decide about their bodies. These achievements have allowed women to have greater autonomy and voice in their relationships, which has transformed the power dynamics between men and women.

<u>Redistribution of responsibilities:</u> The traditional conception of gender roles, in which women were relegated to the domestic sphere and men to the work environment, has been challenged by feminism. Today, men are also expected to actively participate in childcare and household chores. This redistribution has generated a new balance in many couples,

although there are still tensions around traditional expectations and practices that persist.

<u>Transformation in sexual and emotional dynamics:</u> Feminist positions, especially in the third and fourth waves, have advocated for greater openness and understanding of female sexuality, as well as equality in emotional and sexual decision-making. The concept of consent and mutual respect has become paramount in relationships, focusing on open communication and respect for individual boundaries.

Emerging movements and their reactions

<u>The "Men's Rights" movement:</u> As feminist positions gain ground, some movements have emerged in response, such as the "Men's Rights Movement" (MRM), which argues that men's rights have been neglected in favor of women. This movement argues that in areas such as child custody, the judicial system, and education, men face discrimination. These positions generate tensions by introducing a narrative of competition between genders, rather than cooperation for equity.

<u>Emergence of new masculinities:</u> In parallel to critical reactions, a movement has emerged that promotes a revision of traditional masculinities. This approach seeks to free men from the rigid expectations associated with toxic masculinity, such as emotional repression, dominance, and aggression, encouraging empathy, vulnerability, and greater equity in their relationships with women.

<u>Impact of LGBTQ+ movements</u>: The visibility of LGBTQ+ movements has also challenged heteronormative relationships. These movements have broadened the spectrum of what a relationship means and have led to the acceptance of diverse forms of couples and power dynamics. This change has influenced the perception of male-female relationships, demonstrating that the rigidity of gender roles is not necessarily intrinsic or universal.

Current consequences

Although there has been significant progress, there is still resistance to change. Some sectors of society feel uncomfortable with the redefinition of relationships and gender roles. This can lead to friction in interpersonal relationships, especially in couples where one of the partners adheres to more traditional norms while the other identifies with more progressive positions.

Contemporary relationships are facing a rethinking of mutual expectations. Women are no longer looking only for a partner who provides financially, but also one who shares responsibilities and provides emotional support. Men, for their part, are beginning to redefine what it means to be a provider and protector, integrating new sensitivities and skills.

Although many couples today enjoy more equitable relationships than in the past, inequalities persist. Women continue to face wage gaps and a disproportionate burden of domestic work. In addition, forms of gender violence, such as harassment and domestic violence, persist and remain significant obstacles to achieving fully equitable relationships.

Feminist positions and emerging movements have profoundly transformed the relationship between men and women, introducing a focus on equity and mutual respect. However, this process is not free of tensions and challenges. The new dynamics require a constant effort of adaptation and dialogue so that relationships continue to evolve toward greater equality, freedom, and mutual understanding.

Some of the emerging movements are:

1. The Woke Movement and its Connection to Feminism

In recent decades, the term "woke" has gained relevance as a symbol of awareness about social injustices and the fight for equality. Although originally linked to the fight for civil rights and racial justice in the United States, the woke movement has expanded its focus to address a wide range of issues related to social justice, including gender, sexuality, and women's rights. In this context, feminism and the woke movement have found points of convergence, as they both share the goal of challenging and dismantling structures of oppression.

What is the Woke Movement?

The term "woke" comes from the English verb to wake up, and its use began as a metaphor that invites people to stay alert to racial injustices. Over time, the concept was expanded to include greater awareness about the dynamics of power, privilege, and oppression in all its forms. Today, being woke implies having an active commitment to the fight against racism, sexism, homophobia, transphobia, and other forms of discrimination.

Feminism and Woke: Parallel Struggles

Feminism, especially since its third wave, has sought greater intersectionality, recognizing that women are not a homogeneous group and that gender-based oppressions are deeply intertwined with other forms of inequality, such as racism, classism, and homophobia. The intersectional approach to feminism recognizes that the fight for women's rights must include women of different races, classes, sexual identities, and genders.

This approach is aligned with the woke movement, which promotes intersectional awareness. Both movements understand that oppressions do not act in isolation and that the experiences of black, Latina, LGBTQ+, and other minority women are different from those of white women, for example. Therefore, both feminism and the woke movement seek to build a more just and equitable society that is inclusive of all identities.

Tensions between Woke and Feminism

Despite similarities and shared struggles, there are also tensions between feminism and the woke movement. Some branches of feminism, such as radical feminism, have been critical of certain positions taken by the woke movement, particularly about gender and gender identity. The debate over cisgender women's rights versus trans women's rights has been one of the most notable points of friction.

Some radical feminists argue that the woke movement prioritizes struggles for gender identity over the fight for women's rights, which they see as a dilution of the focus on oppression based on biological sex. On the other hand, many woke activists accuse these branches of feminism of being exclusionary and transphobic, failing to fully recognize the rights of trans and non-binary people.

The Impact on Today's Society

The convergence between feminism and the woke movement has had a significant impact on public policies and social debates. Thanks to the awareness promoted by these movements, issues such as sexual harassment, the gender pay gap, and reproductive rights have gained greater visibility. Campaigns such as #MeToo are a clear example of how both movements can come together to address systemic issues of oppression.

Feminism and the woke movement have also promoted critical reflection on traditional gender norms and advocated for the inclusion of all gender identities in feminist spaces. This process of deconstruction has been valuable in advancing understanding of the different ways in which women, and other marginalized people, experience discrimination.

The woke movement and feminism have much in common in terms of their goals of equity and social justice, especially in their intersectional approach to addressing different forms of oppression. Although tensions exist, particularly around issues of gender and sexuality, both movements continue to powerfully influence today's society. Ultimately, their connection lies in the shared commitment to challenging oppressive structures and creating a more inclusive and equitable world for all.

2. The #MeToo Movement: Foundations and Social Significance

The #MeToo movement has been one of the most important phenomena of the last decade in the fight against sexual harassment and gender-based violence. Emerging as a collective call for victims to share their experiences of abuse, this hashtag has transformed the way society, media, and institutions address allegations of sexual violence. Since going viral in 2017, #MeToo has deeply impacted global culture, generating a significant shift in conversations about power, consent, and justice.

Origin of the #MeToo Movement

The origin of the term "Me Too" dates back to 2006, when American activist Tarana Burke first used it to create a space of solidarity and support for women, particularly those from marginalized communities, who had suffered sexual harassment or abuse. The phrase was conceived as a simple and powerful way for victims to share their stories without having to delve into traumatic details, creating a network of empathy and understanding.

However, the movement gained international relevance in October 2017, when actress Alyssa Milano used the hashtag #MeToo on Twitter to invite women to share their experiences of sexual harassment, following public accusations against film producer Harvey Weinstein. Within days, the hashtag went viral and millions of people, women, and men, began sharing their testimonies of abuse, exposing the scope and severity of the problem.

#MeToo Movement Fundamentals

Making Sexual Harassment Visible: One of the main goals of #MeToo is to make sexual harassment and abuse visible, which has long been a taboo subject and often silenced by the victims themselves. By sharing their experiences, people have revealed the omnipresence of harassment in various areas of life, from the workplace to personal relationships.

Breaking the Silence: The strength of #MeToo lies in the ability to break the silence surrounding sexual violence. The movement has provided a platform for victims to feel validated and supported by sharing their stories, creating an environment where society is forced to listen and confront the reality of abuse.

<u>Exposing abuse of power:</u> #MeToo is not just about harassment itself, but the abuse of power that enables it. Many of the initial allegations involved men in positions of authority—from executives and politicians to entertainment figures—using their power to exploit vulnerable people. The movement exposes how power dynamics facilitate abuse and how these structures have protected perpetrators for years.

<u>Empowering victims:</u> One of the fundamental pillars of #MeToo is empowering victims to break the cycle of silence and shame that often surrounds them. The hashtag has allowed many people to find the courage to speak out about their experiences, knowing that they are not alone. The sense of solidarity and collective support has been key to so many voices speaking out.

<u>Cultural and legal change:</u> While cultural change is a central goal of #MeToo, legal reform and accountability are also sought. Public allegations have prompted judicial investigations into those accused of abuse, resulting in convictions and dismissals, and caused institutions and companies to review their policies to prevent harassment.

Global and Cultural Impact of the #MeToo Movement

Since going viral, #MeToo has had a global impact, transcending geographic, cultural, and social boundaries. It has changed the way society perceives sexual harassment and has caused many people to reconsider power dynamics in the workplace, politics, entertainment, and other sectors.

<u>Visibility of gender violence:</u> #MeToo has revealed the magnitude of gender violence and placed it at the center of public conversations. The fact that so many people around the world shared their stories meant that society could not ignore the frequency and severity of the problem.

<u>Revision of work dynamics:</u> In many industries, especially in entertainment, politics, and the media, the movement has forced a review of power structures. Sexual harassment, which was often normalized or covered up, is now being treated more seriously, leading to dismissals, investigations, and changes in internal policies at numerous companies and institutions.

Legal reform: In several countries, #MeToo has prompted legislative reforms aimed at improving protection against sexual harassment. In the United States, for example, there have been efforts to remove confidentiality clauses in employment agreements that allow harassment to be covered up. Laws against sexual violence have also been strengthened, and the creation of safer spaces for victims has been promoted.

<u>Awareness of consent:</u> One of the most profound effects of the movement has been the rethinking of the concept of consent. In many cultures, expectations about relationships between men and women were ambiguous, allowing harassment or coercion to go unnoticed. #MeToo has brought to the table the need for clear, mutual consent in all interactions.

<u>Acceleration of other social movements:</u> The success of #MeToo has inspired other movements related to social justice and equity. It has given rise to other hashtags and campaigns focused on gender equality, women's rights, and justice for marginalized communities, such as #TimesUp and #NiUnaMenos.

Criticisms and Challenges

Despite its positive impact, #MeToo has also faced criticism and challenges. Some people argue that the movement can lead to false accusations or trials without due process. Critics argue that public allegations, especially on social media, can lead to the "cancellation" of people before they are proven guilty. However, #MeToo advocates counter that false accusations are minimal compared to the number of cases of actual harassment that have ultimately come to light.

Another challenge has been the largely white and middle-class focus on women, leading to criticism that the movement does not adequately reflect the experiences of women of color or from less privileged communities. Nonetheless, #MeToo remains a powerful tool for amplifying the voices of oppressed people.

Likewise, the clear line that divides the male approach with romantic intentions from sexual harassment is unclear, causing new generations of men to be reluctant to make a move for fear that their intentions will be mistaken and they will be reported. A clear example of this is the disappearance of the "street compliment".

We can say that the #MeToo movement has had a profound impact on society by making visible and questioning the power dynamics that allow the perpetuation of sexual harassment and abuse. By creating a space for support and solidarity, has allowed victims to talk about their experiences without the stigma that previously silenced them. Although it faces criticism and challenges, #MeToo continues to be a driver of cultural and legal change, driving conversations about consent, power, and justice, and transforming the global landscape regarding gender violence.

3. # I believe you sister: Meaning and Social Significance

The hashtag # I believe you sister has emerged as a powerful symbol of support and sisterhood in the context of the fight against gender violence and sexual abuse. This phrase encapsulates a gesture of credibility and support towards women who report situations of abuse, harassment, or rape, and reflects a transformation in the way society is beginning to deal with these issues.

Beyond being a simple slogan, # I believe you sister has become a social movement that has profound implications for power relations, justice, and the treatment of victims of gender violence.

Origin and Context of the Hashtag

I believe you sister finds its origin in the framework of feminist movements that, in recent decades, have fought against impunity and silence around sexual violence. Inspired by international movements such as #MeToo in the United States, this hashtag is a response to the social and legal distrust that has historically been projected on women who report violence.

For a long time, victims of sexual abuse have been treated with skepticism, facing questioning about their behavior, clothing, or history, which is known as secondary victimization. These types of questions not only reinforce stigmas but also discourage many women from speaking out about their experiences. The emergence of # I believe you sister is an act of resistance to this skepticism, offering a space for validation and empathy.

The Meaning of # I believe you sister

The hashtag has a deep meaning on several levels:

Believing the victims: The heart of the movement is in the unconditional belief in the words of women who report sexual harassment or abuse. In a world where victims are often discredited or doubted, # I believe you sister rejects that culture of suspicion and gives women the benefit of the doubt, breaking the cycle of silence.

<u>Sorority:</u> The word "sister" in the hashtag reinforces the idea of sisterhood, a solidarity between women that transcends the boundaries of race, class, nationality, or religion. This mutual support is vital to counteract the power structures that perpetuate gender violence. # I believe you sister not only reflects empathy but also a call to collective action to confront injustices.

Social denunciation: Beyond personal validation, the hashtag acts as a form of public denunciation against a society that often trivializes or minimizes women's experiences. It is a collective cry that demands that the testimonies of victims be heard, attended to, and, above all, believed.

The Social Significance of #I believe your sister

Cultural transformation: The massive use of # I believe your sister has generated greater awareness about the seriousness of sexual and gender-based violence. It has allowed many stories that were previously kept silent to come to light and has changed the social conversation about it. The media and social networks have become spaces where women can share their experiences without fear of being dismissed.

Impact on the judicial system: The mobilization around this hashtag has also highlighted the shortcomings of the judicial system when dealing with cases of gender-based violence. In many countries, complaints of sexual abuse are often dismissed or treated with indifference, and the legal process for victims is slow and traumatic. The social pressure exerted by movements such as # I believe your sister has driven legislative reforms and increased the demand for a more sensitive and fair approach in cases of violence against women.

Empowerment of women: This hashtag has played a crucial role in the empowerment of women. Knowing that they are not alone, many women have found the courage to speak out about their experiences of abuse or harassment, feeling that their voices will be heard and validated. In this sense, # I believe your sister has allowed many victims to transform their pain into a tool for change.

Change in public perception: Before the emergence of movements such as # I believe your sister, there was a tendency to blame victims or minimize accusations of abuse. The massive use of the hashtag has caused a change in public perception, where there is now a greater willingness to listen to and support victims, rather than doubt or despise them. This has been an important step towards building a culture that condemns abuse and recognizes the importance of believing victims from the beginning.

Generation of support networks: On social media, the hashtag # I believe your sister has allowed support communities to form where women can share their stories without fear of being judged. These networks not only offer emotional solidarity but also provide useful information about legal, psychological, and protection resources, creating a safe space for survivors.

Criticisms and Challenges

Despite its achievements, the # I believe your sister movement has not been without criticism. Some people argue that blindly believing all allegations could lead to false accusations or a lack of fair trial for the accused. However, proponents of the hashtag argue that although cases of false accusations do exist, they are a minority compared to the number of victims who are not believed or supported. For them, the focus should be on correcting the historical distrust towards victims.

I believe your sister is more than just a hashtag; it is a tool for social transformation that has made gender violence visible and created a network of support and solidarity among women. Its impact has resonated both in culture and in legal systems, changing the way society perceives and responds to allegations of abuse. Ultimately, # I believe your sister represents a new way of understanding justice, one that is based on empathy, support, and validation of historically silenced voices.

4. Foundations and Characteristics of the MGTOW Movement (Men Going Their Way)

The MGTOW movement (Men Going Their Way) is a socio-cultural phenomenon that has gained visibility in recent years, especially in online communities. Often described as a philosophy of life, MGTOW focuses on men choosing to disassociate themselves from the traditional expectations and roles that society imposes on them, especially about women and romantic relationships.

Origins of the MGTOW Movement

The MGTOW movement emerged in the early 2000s as a response to what some men perceive as unjust gender dynamics, where laws and social norms favor women over men. While its roots are linked to other men's rights movements, MGTOW is distinguished by a more radical stance that goes beyond fighting for equality in the legal or social realm. Rather than seeking changes in laws or the structure of society, many MGTOW members choose to withdraw from conventional interactions with women and from heteronormative relationships.

Foundations of the MGTOW Movement

One of the ideological foundations of the MGTOW movement is its opposition to what they consider to be radical feminism, which they believe has upset the balance of power between men and women. They argue that laws and cultural norms have disproportionately favored women in areas such as marriage, divorce, child custody, and abuse allegations, leaving men at a disadvantage.

One of the most prominent characteristics of MGTOW is the refusal to engage in romantic or marital relationships. They believe that such relationships are inherently unequal and that men take on more risks and responsibilities without receiving proportional benefits. The concept of women's "detachment" is interpreted as a way to avoid what they perceive as emotional, economic, or legal exploitation.

In turn, the MGTOW movement focuses on male independence, promoting the idea that men should seek their path, without the influences or pressures of society dictating how to live their lives. This includes avoiding emotional or financial commitments that, from their perspective, may put their well-being at risk.

Despite its criticism of conventional interpersonal relationships, MGTOW also emphasizes the importance of self-improvement and personal development. Many members of the movement advocate for men to invest in themselves on a physical, emotional, and financial level, prioritizing their interests and goals over societal demands.

Key Features of the MGTOW Movement

<u>Degrees of Commitment:</u> MGTOW is not a monolithic group, but features different levels of involvement. At the first level, some men simply avoid marriage, but may still maintain occasional romantic relationships. At more advanced levels, some men completely reject any form of relationship with women, opting for a life of total emotional and social independence from them.

<u>Criticism of Traditional Gender Norms:</u> MGTOW followers argue that contemporary social norms still require men to continue to play the roles of providers and protectors in relationships, which they consider unfair. They see these traditional roles as an obstacle to their own freedom and personal development.

<u>Online Communities:</u> The MGTOW movement has found its main base of support in online communities, where men share their experiences, advice, and life philosophies. These virtual spaces act as forums where the ideas of the movement are reinforced and debates about gender dynamics, relationships, and society are encouraged.

<u>Rejection of social expectations:</u> One of the pillars of MGTOW is the rejection of social and cultural expectations that place men under pressure to marry, start a family, and assume traditional roles. MGTOW sees these expectations as a trap that compromises men's freedom and places them in disadvantageous situations in terms of relationships and laws.

Criticisms of the MGTOW Movement

The MGTOW movement has been the subject of criticism from different sectors of society. Many critics point out that the movement reinforces misogynistic attitudes and promotes a negative and distorted view of women and interpersonal relationships. In addition, some experts argue that MGTOW is not a constructive solution to the problems that some men face, since, instead of promoting dialogue and mutual understanding, it encourages withdrawal and isolation.

Feminism, for example, has been a frequent target of MGTOW criticism, but feminist advocates argue that such radical male movements perpetuate gender division rather than seek cooperative solutions for equity.

Nevertheless, the MGTOW movement represents a response to perceived tensions in gender relations in contemporary society. While some see its philosophy as a legitimate form of self-preservation and male empowerment, others criticize it for being a pessimistic and divisive view that reinforces attitudes of distrust and rejection toward women. In any case, MGTOW continues to be a relevant phenomenon within conversations about gender relations and social dynamics, and its impact on contemporary culture remains a topic of debate.

Chapter 10
Toward Mutual Understanding

Feminism and traditional wives have their differences, but they also share common goals, such as the well-being of women and the stability of families. Coming to the end of this book, we will seek to identify these commonalities and explore ways to promote mutual understanding by recognizing and respecting the diversity of women's experiences and life choices.

Recognizing the Diversity of Experiences

The first step toward mutual understanding is to recognize and value the diversity of women's experiences and life choices.

Evolution of Feminism: Since its inception, feminism has evolved to include a variety of perspectives and experiences. More recent waves of feminism have emphasized intersectionality and inclusion.

Traditional Voices: Traditional wives, for their part, have begun to share their stories and experiences, underscoring the importance of their life choices. This recognition of diversity is essential for constructive dialogue.

Commonalities

Despite the differences, there are numerous commonalities between feminism and traditional wives.

Valuing Housework: While feminism has promoted participation in the workforce, it has also recognized the importance of housework and child-rearing. Both groups can come together to fight for recognition and valorization of these tasks.

Autonomy and Choice: Both feminists and traditional wives value autonomy and the ability to choose. The key is to recognize that autonomy can manifest itself in different ways, whether in the home or one's career.

Dialogue and Education

Open dialogue and education are crucial to overcome barriers and foster mutual understanding.

Dialogue Spaces: Creating spaces where feminists and traditional wives can share their experiences and perspectives is essential. These dialogues can help break down stereotypes and foster mutual respect.

Educational Programs: Developing educational programs that include a variety of perspectives on women's roles can help create a more inclusive society. These programs can teach people to value all forms of women's contributions, both at home and in the workplace.

Inclusive Policies

Public policies can play a crucial role in promoting understanding and inclusion.

<u>Family Support:</u> Policies that support families, such as access to childcare services, parental leave, and financial support for homemakers, can benefit both feminists and traditional wives.

<u>Equal Opportunity:</u> Ensuring that all women have equal opportunities to choose their path, whether at home or in the workforce, is a shared goal that can bring both groups together.

Models of Collaboration

There are models of collaboration that have proven effective in promoting understanding and cooperation.

<u>Community Organizations:</u> Some community organizations have been successful in bringing together women from different perspectives to work on common projects, such as supporting motherhood and advocating for women's rights.

<u>Global Movements:</u> Global movements such as HeForShe have promoted gender inclusion and cooperation, offering a model for how feminists and traditional wives can work together toward common goals.

<u>Local Initiatives</u>: In some communities, local initiatives have been successful in bringing together women from different backgrounds to work on projects of common interest, such as improving maternal health services and creating support networks for mothers.

The path to mutual understanding between feminists and traditional wives is not without its challenges, but it is possible. By recognizing and respecting the diversity of life experiences and choices, fostering dialogue and education, and promoting inclusive policies, a more just and respectful society for all women can be built. This chapter has explored pathways towards this goal, highlighting the importance of mutual respect and cooperation in the fight for equality and well-being for all women.

_____0_____